The Splendor of Mother & Child Animals

An Emma Rose Sparrow Book

Publish Date: November 15, 2015

Editor-in-Chief: Connor Chagnon
Sterling Elle Publishing
Bradford, Massachusetts

ISBN-13: 978-1519333315
ISBN-10: 1519333315

Photo Credits

The artist/source credits for the photos in this book are listed in the order in which they appear:

Made in the USA
Lexington, KY
09 May 2018